Mindful Sales

What's that?

IDK - that's why I'm reading the book!

Oh 🤭

Barbara Zirkelbach
Adolfo Soberanis

Mindful Sales

Copyright © 2020 by Barbara Zirkelbach and Adolfo Soberanis

Edited by Helen Wilson

Cover Photo by Adolfo Soberanis
Copyright © 2018 Adolfo Soberanis
Back Cover Photo by Salome Szecsei
Copyright © 2018 Salome Szecsei

All rights reserved. No part of this book may be reproduced in any form or by any means, electronic or mechanical, without the written permission of the authors, except by a reviewer, who may quote
passages in a review. Any person or institution who wishes to use part of all of this book for
educational or other purposes, photocopy part or all of this book or include the book in any type of anthology can request permission by sending an inquiry to:

Adolfo Soberanis
P.O. Box 5717
Eureka, CA.
        95502

Print ISBN: 978-0-692-18555-1
EPUB ISBN: 978-0-692-04172-7

Mindful Sales
Contents

I.	Wake Up!	4
II.	Mindfulness	6
III.	Learning Curves	9
IV.	Ad Space	14
V.	Job Landing	18
VI.	The Core	24
VII.	Caretaking	30
VIII.	Out of Bounds	36
IX.	The Stance	39
X.	In Focus	41
XI.	The Comfort Zone	45

A personal touch...

This book is *your* book. It's for you. Before you begin, here's a true story from Barbara's life:

Selling cars is a tough business. One day a woman came into the dealership where Barbara worked and wanted to look at some cars. The woman was shy and quiet and didn't seem like she actually had the real desire or money to buy a car. Barbara didn't focus on those things. She showed the woman the cars that interested her, treated her with kindness, gave her a lot of information and sincerely wished her well when she left.

The next day the woman returned and bought a brand new car. She told Barbara, "You know, I went to every dealership to find a car and I came back here because you didn't push me, you just helped. I didn't feel judged. I felt like you just cared about what I needed. So, thank you for that."

That set in motion Barbara's quest to help sales people to become more caring and less forceful. Sales people who just want to help connect customers with the right product to meet their needs.

That woman came back and bought a new car from Barbara every few years because Barbara had been mindful, compassionate, and aware.

This book is the continuation of that experience. It's here to help you. We hope that you enjoy it!

Sincerely,

Barbara Zirkelbach
&
Adolfo Soberanis

Mindful Sales

Chapter 1

Wake Up!

It's Monday.

    The alarm screams in your ear, "**Get up!**" Your eyes don't want to open, your body begs for five more minutes of sleep, and your hand mindlessly kills the alarm. You know that you can't go back to sleep. You have to get to work on time and have the energy of a chihuahua and the teeth of a cheetah to get through the day. You pull yourself up out of bed, groggily go through the morning routine and slowly wake up with the help of some coffee.

    You get in your car and, while driving to work, the radio blasts messages that try to get you to buy a product, a service, or a way of thinking. You hear an ad for a podcast and a pop-star is going to be talking about her experiences with meditation. You're interested but wonder when you'd have the time to listen. I mean, life is busy, right?

Mindful Sales

Your mind wanders and you begin to wonder why so many people, including doctors, researchers, teachers, movie stars and others are talking about this thing called, "mindfulness". What is it, exactly, and why are so many people talking about it?

The morning commute blurs into memory and your work station becomes your mind. Customers, tasks and co-worker issues keep you busy until the time clock tells you to go. Before you know it you're back in your car, the radio a steady stream of background noise, and your mind wanders.

The stress from the day pulls at your neck and shoulders. The million things that you have to do never seem to end. You complete one task and another pops up to take its place. It's easy to feel overwhelmed and just plain "fed up" with all of life's concerns. You need a respite but vacations are few and far between and very expensive. Plus, they don't really help to deal with stress on a day to day basis, do they? You need a remedy that no pill can provide, so your mind goes back, again, to this whole idea of mindfulness and meditation.

Maybe you've never heard of it before. Maybe people at work talk about it but you've never tried it or really don't understand what they're talking about. None of that matters. What matters is that you have this book and this opportunity to relieve some of the day to day stress and help people. This is a chance to make all of that happen and make your work day more fun, more productive and less stressful by actually putting in less effort! That sounds counterintuitive, but it's not. It works - and all you have to do is practice.

Chapter 2

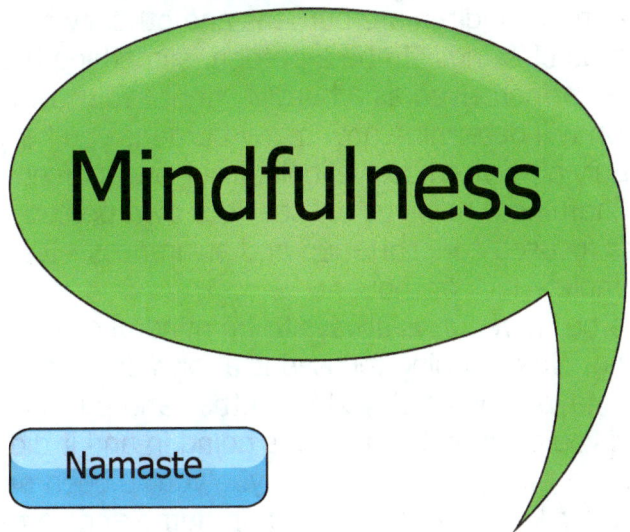

Mindfulness

Namaste

Remember this word – "Namaste" (Nah-mahs-tay). You may have heard it before, or seen it in traffic on a bumper sticker, but do you know what it means? Loosely translated, it means, "I recognize the divine in you and it's the same as the divine in me." Remember that as you face each customer, each person in your life – even your own self - there is something divine in all of Life. Now, let's take a minute to understand mindfulness.

It's simple, really, and you have been mindful many, many times in your life. Your entire first few years were spent in a state of deep mindfulness as you focused entirely on learning to walk and talk. You were a baby and baby's are born mindful! Baby "you" didn't notice many other things around you and stayed very focused on walking and talking until they became "second nature". Now, you walk and talk effortlessly. Mindfulness makes things seem effortless.

Mindful Sales

Concentration on the moment relieves many burdens.

Burdens have to be "thought of" to exist. You can't buy one in the store. We've all met parents who think that their chidlren are burdens and others who see them as blessings. To be a burden, something has to be seen or perceived as a burden, right? Your own perception will determine how many burdens you have in life. But, how often do we look at our own perceptions? Mindfulness helps us to "see" our own perceptions. It's focused concentration and awareness. It's not a complete lack of thought.

To be "mindful" is always to be mindful of something. Just keeping focused is a form of mindfulness. Maybe you've played basketball and put up a shot that you absolutely knew was going in and it did – that was a mindful moment! Maybe you've been on a mountain bike ride and every bump, jump and corner smoothly rolled by under your tires. It was so great that you didn't even notice how long it took. That was a mindful bike ride. You've probably even done it at work – gotten into the groove and just paid attention to what needed to be done and, suddenly, it was time to go home. The "easy" days are the "mindful" days.

The human mind likes to wander. It thinks about the past, the future, bills that need to be paid, dream vacations, people we love or miss and so much else. Those things only exist in the mind and too often take us away from whatever we're doing at the moment. There's always a time and a place for thinking about those things but when you're in the middle of helping someone at work it really helps to simply let those thoughts go for a little while. Meditation is one way of practicing mindfulness when things are calm. It's like baseball practice, learning to play and instrument, or dance practice. There's no pressure to get things right. Some people take the time to mediate so that they can stay mindful when things are difficult or stressful. Science has shown that mediation turns the "thinking" part of the brain on and turns the "fight or flight" part of the brain off. That's why doctors, pain clinics and superstars are using mindfulness and mediation. It works and it doesn't have to be done in a temple or anywhere specific but it does help to practice in quiet, comfortable places like a bedroom or living room.

Once you get some practice, you'll find that you can "meditate" at a stop light, in line at the grocery store or while you're waiting for the doctor to call you in for your appointment. It's not magic. It's just something that you can do, like riding a bike or paying a bill. It's thinking about what you ARE doing at any given moment and nothing else. If you have something else on your mind, that's okay - just learn to let it go in that moment and think about it when you get home or when you have the time. Put all of your attention on the task or person in front of you. That's it, really. It just takes practice.

Mindfulness is just about being present. Be there for the person in front of you. Be there for yourself. Be there each moment because there is nothing else. The past is only memories in the mind and the future is just ideas of what might happen or come to be. If you take care of the present moment then the future is also taken care of and the past is more easily accepted and understood. So, it's pretty simple, right? Just be yourself, alive and awake in the only time that actually exists – this moment. This is your alarm. **Wake up!**

Mindful Sales

Chapter 3

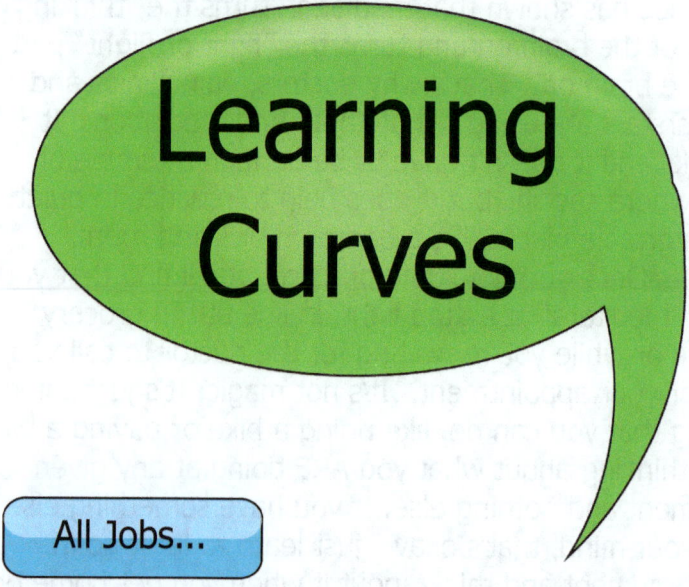

Learning Curves

All Jobs...

...require some basic skills. Other sales strategies may focus on "closing" or on aggressive tactics. This book is focused on being mindful of the product and the customer; therefore, the basic skills are slightly different. Selling in a mindful way, the basic skills include product knowledge, listening, understanding and interaction.

Product knowledge is very important. How can a doctor help you when you're sick if the doctor doesn't have any knowledge of illnesses or treatments? How can a teacher help you to learn algebra if she can't do basic math? In that same vein of thinking, how can a salesperson help a customer find the right product if the sales person has no knowledge of the products? We've already gone through some tips about how to be awake, aware and mindful, now let's look at some of the important things to know about products.

Mindful Sales

1. General information – be sure that you know at least the general information about the product, such as brand name, country of origin and what it does.
2. Company information – it helps to know something about the company that created the product. Is it a "green" company? Is it based in San Francisco or Tokyo? Do they donate proceeds to charity or support local schools? Is it public or private? Do they stand by their products with a great warranty program for customers? This type of information can make customers feel more comfortable knowing that they're supporting a company that upholds their own, individual beliefs about business, fair trade, etc. Just remember, it's not your job to judge - just to pass along the information. Keep your professional boundaries.
3. Product functionality – learn how the product works. Use the display model, ask a manager if one can be opened and "tinkered" with or find a friend who has one that you can use. Discover what it does, how it works and how well it works. Find out what it can and can't do – what the product's limitations are – and think about unique, "life-hacking" possibilities for the product.
4. Warranty – many customers want to know what the warranty is on expensive products so be sure to learn about the warranty. What is covered and not covered? How long is it covered? What is the warranty process – does the customer go through the store where it was originally purchased or through the manufacturer? Knowing these things will help your customers to feel comfortable when making their purchase.

Above all, be honest with customers. Tell them what you know and, if you don't know something, tell them that you don't know but you'll find out. Whenever possible – go and find them an answer. Even if you don't, they'll appreciate the effort because they will feel heard.

Listening is another important tool to keep in your box. Anybody with working ears can hear but listening is a skill. Listening requires understanding. They can't be separated. For example, you go to the doctor and say, "Doc, my knee hurts." If the doctor listens then she'll examine your knee and everything closely connected to it. If the doctor hears you, but doesn't listen, she might ask you how your vision is or how your arm is feeling. Then, you might get frustrated and tell her that your knee is the problem. She will hear you speaking but won't understand what you're saying until she actually listens. It's the same in sales. If a customer needs a lawnmower and you show her screwdrivers then she's likely to get frustrated and be uncomfortable. If you ask her how big her lawn is, if she needs a riding mower or a push mower or if she'd like to see the new battery powered mower then she'll know you were listening and that you're interested in getting her the product that she needs. She will feel understood.

Understanding is a key component of being helpful. Once you really listen to the customer then you will either know a possible product that the customer can use or you can ask what are called "clarifying questions". Clarifying questions, such as, "How big is your lawn?" or, "Do you prefer gas or electric?" can help you to understand what the customer wants and/or needs. The customer might want a riding mower, but after asking a few clarifying questions you learn that he lives in a rural area and that he doesn't have a lawn, just a plot of very rugged land. Riding mowers, you know from product research, don't work well on rugged land so you may suggest a gas or battery powered string trimmer. You'll be able to explain that he can choose a riding mower but that it will often break down due to hitting rocks, clumps of dirt and sticks from the trees on his property while a high-quality string trimmer will last for years and not be affected by any of the things that can ruin a riding mower. A more informed sales person creates a more informed customer. That customer will then tell his friends how helpful and knowledgeable you are and will return the next time he needs to buy something for his property – like a chainsaw or a rototiller. You listened, understood his needs and guided him to the right product. That was the end result of a healthy interaction!

    Interactions are a key to any type of relationship. The relationship between a sales person and a customer is no different. When interacting with customers it's important for the sales person to have a friendly demeanor, to be non-judgmental and to be patient. Greeting the customer in a helpful, friendly manner and acknowledging the customer as a person is very important. This person may need your help to make a good decision. Keep the interaction professional and friendly. Engage the customer in relevant conversation about the product or what it's going to be used for and do your best to avoid politics or personal issues. There are always customers who will want to discuss their angst about products made in China or how their relative used a certain product in the wrong way and how "stupid" people are, etc. Listen and then steer the conversation back to the present moment – what that customer needs at that time. Guide the conversation and keep it as focused as possible.

For example, Maria comes in and wants some nursing shoes. While fitting her she tells you, "I hate those old, stinky men who come into the hospital. They're so demanding."
What do you do? How do you acknowledge her feelings but not get involved?

You could say, "I hear ya. Demanding people can be a challenge. Does that shoe fit? Would you like to try the other one?
Or, you could say, "I understand. I hope that these new shoes will bring you some relief. Do they fit?"

There are many ways to respond. Find what works for you - what feels natural. Focus on what the customer needs and it'll be easier to keep them focused on their needs, too. Once you understand what the customer needs, then there is a next possible step to an interaction.

Interacting with the product is a great way to help customers get a feel for whether or not the product will work for them. Let them "experience" it. If you sell wheelchairs and a customer comes in who can't use his legs at all and only his left arm has any movement then you must find an electric chair with left hand controls. Help the customer to sit in the chair and ensure that it fits his body and that the controls are within reach. Have him try to manipulate the chair using the controls. Ask how the chair feels to him. If you're selling cars, then take the customer on a test drive. Demonstrations can help, but actual interactions with products are very powerful to help ensure happy customers.

Mindful Sales

Chapter 4

Ad Space

Understanding...

...advertising and concepts like brand loyalty are also important to sales people. Remember, it's the understanding that's important – whether it's understanding what the person needs, what her concerns are, how a product works or how advertising works in the mind and why people remain loyal to certain brands – understanding is still the key to unlocking your own potential to be helpful and effective. Brand loyalty drives certain customers, especially car buyers, while the repetition and content of advertisements can influence others. Brand loyalty is that thing that drives people to purchase products from the same company over and over again. Some people, for example, only buy Chevrolet trucks or Pampers diapers. It doesn't matter to them what the competitors in that same market say or do – they are loyal to the brand.

Some people become unhappy with a certain brand after even just one bad experience. Customers wanting to switch brands will need a lot of information to put them into their comfort zone. Brand loyalty is critical to a business because it not only means returning customers, but the business also gains free advertising through word-of-mouth and online reviews. For the sales person, however, knowing what brand a customer is loyal to is nothing to judge – it's just more information that can be used to help the customer get what she wants or needs. It's nothing personal. People loyal to a certain brand will usually tell you right away and those who want to change will also usually tell you that they're unhappy with brand X and want to try something new. Those people, and people with no brand loyalty, are the ones who will really benefit from and appreciate your knowledge, experience, and expertise about the products you sell. They need more than a radio, print or T.V. ad can give them.

Advertising works in the mind in interesting ways. Repetition is very important in advertising, for example, because it helps to put images, jingles and slogans into the long-term memory portion of the consumer's mind. Once it's stored in the long-term memory, the brand becomes easily recognizable in the store and viewed by the consumer as something that they already know and trust – even if they've had no experience with that brand or product. Many customers who enter your sales life will have had vast amounts of exposure to advertising. Some will outright believe the ads and others will be more skeptical and have questions about the product. Help them by knowing how a company advertises, what it advertises, who the target market of its ad campaigns is and what message the

Mindful Sales

company is sending. Every company sends a message. Ford wants you to think that their trucks are tough. Huggies wants you to think that new parents prefer their brand. Every company is fighting for a piece of the pie that you're actually serving. Stay out of the fight and remain focused on helping. Whatever brand the customer wants, whatever product the customer is looking for is fine, as long as you can help them get what they're after. The newest forms of advertising are a bit more elusive, such as social media campaigns, viral videos and ads placed strategically in feeds like Instagram.

With the advent of computers and smart phones, advertising has become more invasive and prominent. Instead of just seeing a couple of billboards on the way to work, hearing ads every once in a while on the radio or while flipping through a magazine at a doctor's office, ads are now a part of our social lives. They pop-up on Instagram, Facebook and Twitter in-between the messages, posts and pics from our friends, families and associates. The images and messages from our social lives are now being intermingled with messages from Johnson & Johnson, Southwest Airlines and Amazon, to name a very few. Advertisers are reaching children who never would have been exposed to such ads, they're touching the parts of our mind where we care about others and it's creating a new consumer consciousness. These ads are so powerful, in fact, that the U.S. government is looking deeply into how they may have impacted the 2018 presidential elections.

That goes beyond propaganda and enters the realm of mental manipulation. As a sales person, it's important to be aware that you are also bombarded with these ads and reflect on how they affect your own notions, your ideas, your friends and family, what you like or don't like, what you buy and your very thoughts. Simply be aware that others are also being affected by this in new ways that have not yet been studied. Advertising affects all of us in different ways and you will begin to see consumers who are more aware, more educated about products and, simultaneously, confused.

The new methods of advertising can bring about new awareness but also a bit of confusion in the minds of consumers. People are beginning to ask themselves where their money is going and how honest a company is about their products. This type of awareness is a type of mindfulness. Mindful of what is being consumed. This type of thinking prompted actress Jessica Alba to start The Honest Company. She didn't feel like she could be sure about the sourcing or the integrity of companies producing food for her children and so she started a business that allowed her to feel safe and promotes that same feeling of security to other parents around the world. Advertising itself is not good or bad, it just is, and we need to be aware of how it is affecting ourselves and the people we serve.

Mindful Sales

Chapter 5

Job Landing

Applying...

...for jobs can be a job in itself. A great application starts with a great resumé. Some people know how to write a resume´ and others hire people or businesses to write a resume for them. Here are few tips on how to write a great resumé:
1. Use a template! Microsoft Word and other word processing programs like OpenOffice have templates that you can use that will make your resumé look great.
2. List your jobs from present or most recent to first and go up to fifteen years back.
3. List your dates of employment, supervisor name and contact information.
4. Provide specific details of what you did while employed. Instead of just saying, "cashier", write, "customer service, used P.O.S. machine, handled merchandise sales and returns" – these details will make

you look good!   *Mindful Sales*

Once your resumé is done, you'll often need a cover letter. Some people choose to write generic cover letters and then just change the name of the business that they're applying to but we suggest that you take the time to write individual cover letters. Focus on what each employer has asked for in their job posting and address how you can meet their needs. Having hired a lot of people over the years, we know that the cover letter needs to catch the employer's eye and not waste his or her time. Avoid telling about personal information, like what you do in your spare time, unless it relates to the position. For example, talking about your favorite pet when applying for a job at a pet store only works if you stay focused on how you care for that pet, what you've learned about animals in general and how to sell pet supplies. Just saying that you love your cat is not enough. A cover letter needs to be focused on what skills and experience you can bring to the business.

Cover letters, like business, are always evolving. Adaptation is the key to success in today's globalized workforce. There are still traditional business models that want to see a very succinct, almost sterile cover letter. We are seeing, however, that many start-ups and new ventures want to break that model and specifically ask applicants to write a different kind of cover letter. We're giving you two examples here, along with fictional job postings, to illustrate what we're seeing in the marketplace. The first posting is for Parson Education and they want a more traditional cover letter. The second is for an internet based start-up and they want something new and different.

Mindful Sales

1. Parson Education is looking for a curriculum developer. We want a talented art teacher with at least three years of teaching experience. Curriculum design is a plus but will teach the right candidate. Please send a brief cover letter of your experience and anything that you specialize in.

ANGELA SANTINO
EDUCATION/CREATIVE | HTTPS://ANGSAN.MYPORTFOLIO.COM/

CONTACT

P.O. Box 1111
Tilted Creek, CA. 95533
angsan31@mail.com
580.689.3881

PARSON EDUCATION

SUNNY VIEW, CA.

03.05.18

Dear Parson Education,

I have a B.A. in Art Education and have taught art for the past five years at The Language Acadamy in Tilted Creek, CA. I specialize in digital art and am proficient in pottery, watercolor and acrylic painting. My students have gone on to attend the Academy of Fine Arts and other renowned institutions. I teach traditional art classes and classes for artistically gifted and talented youth.

My current professional goal includes creating curriculum and bringing public school art programs into the information age. Working in schools I found that the materials and curriculum needed to be enhanced so that my students would have the skills necessary to attend higher institutions and compete in the global workforce. I have created hundreds of projects and lesson plans to accomplish that goal and have been highly successful. I would like to bring my skills and experience to Parson Education and work together to enhance the current curriculum.

I look forward to the opportunity to interview and collaborate on new concepts.

Sincerely,
Angela Santino

EMAIL   TWITTER HANDLE   TELEPHONE   LINKEDIN URL

2. EdStomp.com is hiring! We want a Jedi art teacher to use the Force and help us to find new ways to bring art education to the next generation. The internet models for education haven't taken off and traditional models are floundering. Write us a sharp, witty, funny or just creative cover letter that will show us your personality and tell us if you're game to change the game!

ANGELA SANTINO
EDUCATION/CREATIVE | HTTPS://ANGSAN.MYPORTFOLIO.COM/

CONTACT

P.O. Box 1111
Tilted Creek, CA. 95533
angsan31@mail.com
580.689.3881

EDSTOMP.COM

SUNNY VIEW, CA.

03.05.18

Dear EdStomp.com,
I'm game! Let's get these kids terraforming planets and using "The Force"!
The director of schools in Finland said that we Americans are, basically, "stupid" for not implementing the findings of OUR OWN research into schools and he's right! I can see that EdStompt is positioned to change that and I'm all in.
If you don't know who Alexander Von Humboldt was, well, that's part of the problem. If you don't know what he did for the world then get a hold of me and I'll tell you. We can incorporate his approach, inspired by Goethe, to move beyond the boring and create something even hotter than S.T.E.A.M.!

I live in Northern California and could attend quarterly meetings or travel to Sunny View when necessary. I'm very computer literate and have a stable, high speed internet connection. I'm reliable, hard-working and highly motivated to learn and grow.

I hope to hear from you and look forward to being able to communicate in person. Feel free to pound me with questions about Child Development, positive guidance, writing, art, pedagogical techniques or anything else that bakes your cookies.

Sincerely,
Angela Santino

EMAIL

TWITTER HANDLE

TELEPHONE

LINKEDIN URL

Mindful Sales

The examples above are both appropriate cover letters but each one is tailored to the needs, requests and desires of each business. Be sure to make your cover letter look great, be easy to read and meet the requirements and requests of the business that you're applying to and you'll often land an interview!

Interviewing is always nerve wracking but it becomes pleasurable, even fun, when you're mindful. Being mindful of who you are, aware of your skills and your limitations allows you to own the interview. Walk in, greet the person or panel with confidence and answer the questions honestly. The confidence that you carry into the room, unlike traditional ideas of having confidence that you'll get the job, is actually confidence that you know yourself, you're aware of what you can do and that your goal is to help the company and the customers. It's a confidence in selflessness and in understanding. A confidence in being able to learn, cooperate and listen. It has nothing to do with imagining that you're the best or that you're going to get the job and everything to do with understanding that you'll do your best and you're going to be honest. So, be confident, be honest and do your best. We have always landed jobs this way so we know that it works.

Here's a great example:

Adolfo was in college, working part-time at a school but wanted another part-time job so that he could limit the amount of student loans that he needed to finish school. He decided that he would like to work at the local library. It would give him a quiet place to work and help him to access more resources for school as well as put him in a position to help others who came to the library to learn.

So, he walked into the library one day and simply asked if they had any positions open. They did. He immediately filled out the application, wrote a coverletter and turned them both in. He was then interviewed, took a quick test on alphabetizing and the Dewey decimal system and was hired. He had NEVER worked in a library before but he was confident that he could learn what he didn't know and that he would be a helpful employee. They hired him because of the immediate action he took when the application was handed to him, his ability to pass the simple tests and his confidence that he could learn and help. It also helped him to keep my student loans low, borrowing about half of what his peers borrowed to complete the same degree.

That job was not in sales but it was in the area of service. He helped hundreds, if not thousands, of people find the information that they needed, books that they liked and he learned how to access resources that he never knew existed – especially online databases. This experience helped him immensely when he did get into the retail sector because he knew how to research and find out information that would help customers to make informed purchases. He landed the job that led to the accumulation of knowledge that helped him to get managerial and business consulting jobs. You can do the same.

Landing a job requires only being aware of yourself, having a clean and attractive resumé and creating individualized cover letters. Be honest, dress appropriately and show up early. Those things alone will set you apart from many other candidates, helping you to land a job that you'll love!

Mindful Sales

Chapter 6

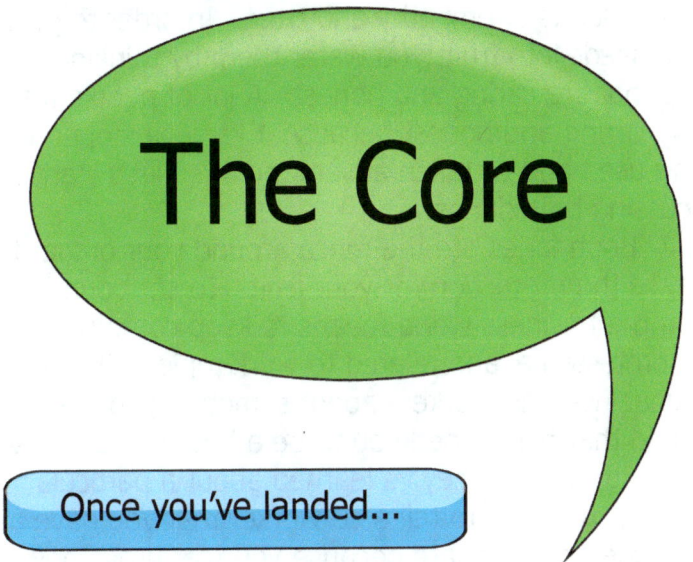

The Core

Once you've landed...

...a job then it's time to start selling! At the core of sales is something that most people don't expect to find. Not knowing what the "core" is has given sales people the stereotype of being "sleazy", "greedy" or "pushy". Imagine an apple. It looks good on the outside and it might taste good but the core is the most important part of the apple. Without the core, there would be no seeds to create new apple trees and, thus, new apples. It's the apple's core that holds the essential aspects of an apple – right there in the seeds – everything needed to grow a tree and thousands of apples. We all have seeds inside of us – seeds of anger, greed, hatred and envy but also seeds of compassion, kindness, caring, humility and happiness. The seeds that we water are the seeds that will grow. It's that simple. So, what seeds will be at the core of YOU – as

Mindful Sales

a human being and a sales person?

The seeds that we have seen, over and over again, that produce sales and happy, returning customers, are seeds of empathy and trust. In order to grow these seeds into fruit, you water them by thinking in ways that are caring and honest. A lot of people fear being caring and honest because it leaves us open to being used and/or taken advantage of so let's start by discussing boundaries.

Boundaries are the fence around your orchard. They're the protection for your fruit. To set boundaries in the business world means to keep communication professional and related to work topics. It's okay to "chat" with co-workers about something you've learned that has helped you to be a better sales person or something that they've learned about a particular product. It's okay to tell a co-worker that you have a headache or you're late because your car broke down but avoid taking personal conversation any farther than that. We have experienced the reality that it is very difficult for people to set boundaries after working together for extended periods of time. People get to know each other, regardless of the work environment. The point is to keep work at work and home at home as much as is humanly possible.

One store that Adolfo managed had a very challenging staff when he first took the position. The former manager had no idea how to set boundaries and so certain staff members walked all over him, disrespected him and did whatever they wanted to, when they wanted to, regardless of what needed to be done. Customers were very unhappy with the service that they received and the owner was extremely frustrated because sales were down. Instead of firing the current

Mindful Sales

manager, Adolfo suggested that they keep him on, use his skills to help and just give him a new position within the company. The owner agreed and Adolfo put him in charge of fulfilling special orders and completing regular orders for re-stocking merchandise. The employee no longer had to work with the public regularly and no longer had to try to control the employees. He did well at his new post and kept it for many years!

One employee, in particular, was really at the heart of the store's issues. She wore clothes that accentuated her figure and spent a lot of her money on hair and nails. She focused more on her looks than her core. She consistently brought her personal drama into the workplace. She took lunch when she wanted to and returned when she wanted to, regardless of the schedule or other people's needs. She dumped her problems on customers and rarely asked what they needed or how she could help. Instead of putting her efforts into helping, she spent a lot of time trying to manipulate people into hating or disrespecting others - those whom she believed deserved it because they'd done her "wrong" somehow. Adolfo remained true to his core, never talked bad about her and always treated her with respect and kindness, so everything that she did backfired on her.

The other staff began to distance themselves from her as they realized that he was managing from a stance of support and that he "walked the talk". He showed them, day after day, that he was supporting them in getting their jobs done and ensuring that they had the resources, training and time needed to complete their tasks. He provided regular trainings, brought reps in to educate staff on products, had "pizza parties", and always followed through on his promises to get something done. The staff began to respect him and to reject her. Losing that false sense of control was so emotionally devestating to her, something that she had depended on for her identity, that he didn't even have to fire her. Less than three weeks after he took the management position, she quit. Sadly, she didn't know how to fit into an atmosphere of kindness and honesty.

He hired a very honest, hard-working young man to take her place and he worked at that store for four years. When he left for the police academy, they hired his younger sister. Customer satisfaction skyrocketed, we hit fifth in the nation for sales of a very expensive brand of pocket knife and staff stayed with us for an average of three or more years. Most of our staff were college students, so it is quite a success to keep them for that many years.

Training the sales associates always began with a conversation about being helpful. It was imperative to the business that people felt helped. We often referred people to other stores if we didn't carry what they needed – even calling the other stores to see if they had the item in stock and how much it cost. Customer ratings online went from two stars when Adolfo started to five stars within six months. This isn't rocket science – it's just mindfulness – awareness of and compassion for the person in front of you (within professional boundaries, of course).

Setting boundaries in a mindful way is a key to success. The staff of that store were allowed to chat amongst themselves and encouraged to engage customers in conversations about their needs. They were lauded for providing product information and being honest and helpful. They bonded and formed friend ships outside of work but kept their personal lives away from the store. Boundaries work with staff but they also must be set, and kept, with the customer.

Setting boundaries with customers is as easy as saying, "I hear you but that's another conversation." Or, "I understand. Does that shoe feel alright?" Customers will sometimes try to drag you into conversations about politics, religion or other socially sensitive topics.

We all have our ideas and opinions in those areas but be mindful that the customer is there to fulfill a need and the only thing that you can teach them in that place, at that time, is about the products. It's okay to tell a story about how that particular flashlight worked so great the last time you went camping or how that model of truck has pulled your friend's trailer well for five years. Try not to go any further than that. The customer doesn't need to know what happened on your camping trip. If the customer asks, "What did you do on that camping trip?" simply respond that you had a good time, or you hiked for two days and then talk about what the customer needs.

"I hiked for two days and that flashlight worked great! Do you need a really bright light to see things far away or do you want more of a 'task' light that just lights up an area about twenty feet in front of you?" These simple ways of communicating set boundaries and still allow you to be yourself and keep your core alive.

Keeping the core alive also requires direct communication. Direct communication kills the seeds of manipulation and dishonesty. It supports truth and helpfulness. That doesn't mean tell a customer, "Your breath stinks!" Instead, it means be direct when they

Mindful Sales

ask you a question about a product. If you don't know the answer, tell them that you don't know and then go find a manager, co-worker or product manual to help find the answer. That shows the customer that you're honest and that you care. Communicating directly and honestly with your customer will build trust and they will want to return again and again because they feel comfortable and safe.

Remember, whatever seeds you water are what will grow inside of you. Watering the seeds of integrity will help you to create trust and successful business r elationships. Setting boundaries with co-workers and customers will ensure that the work place is safe and comfortable for everybody and clear, direct communication will help everybody to understand and to feel understood. These are the core aspects of sales. Take care to remember and implement them and you'll be successful.

Mindful Sales

Chapter 7

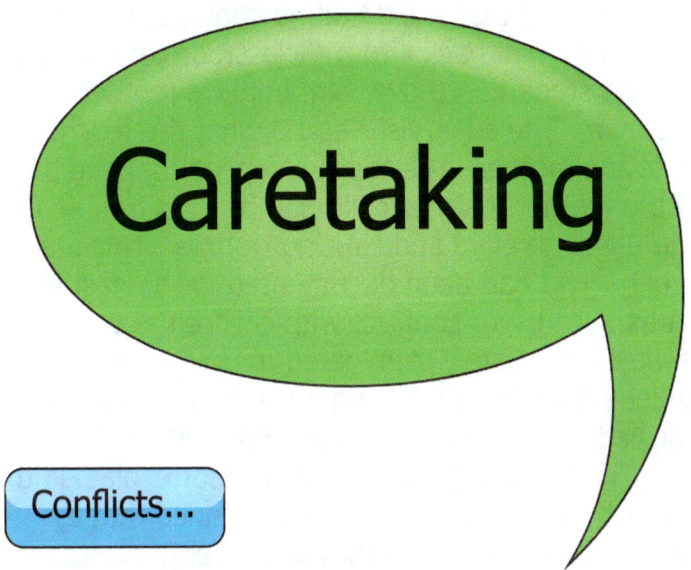

Caretaking

Conflicts...

...will inevitably arise in the workplace. Some conflicts will happen between co-workers and some will happen between customers and sales people. They are a very important part of life. Conflict creates opportunities for us to learn and grow. They are the dirt in your orchard. Without dirt, there can be no apple trees. We need the dirt of life, with all of its bacteria and organisms, to grow the food that keeps us healthy. If we can learn to "fight fair" and see conflict as healthy, we lose our fear of it and can begin to use it to grow.

One day a teacher picked up a child who had run out of her classroom, threw him on her shoulder, and carried him back into the class. The supervisor saw the event through a window and approached the teacher after class. He asked her why she had thrown the child, kicking and screaming, over her shoulder. She told him that the child had refused to clean up and, when she tried to punish him with a "time-out", he ran out onto the playground.

She said that she'd had no choice but to pick him up and carry him back into the classroom, put him in a chair and stand guard over him until his mother came to get him. The supervisor asked what the teacher had said to the mother. The teacher replied that she had told the mother that her child had been in trouble for being uncooperative and causing trouble. This teacher's behaviors had been documented for the last two months because of conflicts with children and parents. She was immediately terminated for her actions. Can you understand why? How did she handle conflict? What had she done that was so unacceptable?

The first thing that the supervisor explained to her was that all teachers had been trained that they only pick a child up when they are a danger to themselves or others and then they are to be picked up from behind, under the arms. That is the safest way for both parties involved. Next, the supervisor reminded her about the other ways to resolve conflict that they'd discussed over the last few months. She couldn't remember them because she hadn't paid close attention and then watered the seeds of compassion and understanding in herself. Instead, she'd chosen to continue to water the seeds of anger and frustration. For clarity, the supervisor reminded her that anger was fear and frustration happened when we lacked a tool or ability to do something. She'd been given the tools and she had chosen not to use them, so conflict continued in the classroom.

It took two weeks to hire a new teacher. During that time the supervisor taught the class. The child

Mindful Sales

who had been picked up and punished began, the first day, by taking toys from other kids and then running around the classroom and taunting them. When the assistant teacher tried to stop him by chasing him around the classroom and asking him to stop he simply ran faster, laughed and mocked her. The supervisor observed this behavior and decided to try a different approach. He saw that the conflict was not occurring during the morning circle, when they sang songs and got ready for the day, but only during "free" time. So, he called all of the children to circle and said that it was a "special" circle, recognizing that they didn't normally have circle that time of day.

The children all sat down and wriggled and chatted and laughed. The supervisor did nothing. He just sat still and watched the children. It only took about thirty seconds for a couple of the children to realize that the teacher wasn't doing anything. They immediately began to ask the other kids to be quiet and to look at the supervisor. He continued to sit quietly. Soon, the whole class was silent and staring at the supervisor. None of them knew how to react to silence.

The supervisor remained quiet, took a tray that he'd prepared ahead of time and set it in front of him. He then took the items off of the tray, named them one by one, then demonstrated what to do with them and how to put them neatly back on the tray. The children paid very close attention to the supervisor because he did not create conflict within their minds. He knew that pre-school aged children could either comprehend language or action so he limited his language and allowed them to focus on his actions. That eliminated the conflict in their minds about what to focus on. No conflict, no problems.

Then, he switched to language and put all of the objects that might draw their attention away. He told the children that the classroom was their classroom and that he just worked there to help them. He said that it was too big of a job to keep it clean all by himself and asked if they could help him. They all nodded in agreement. He also admitted, honestly, that he didn't know where everything was in the classroom since he hadn't been their regular teacher and asked the child who had been carried and punished if he could "show him where everything goes". The child agreed with a smile and the teacher dismissed the kids.

That boy eagerly showed the supervisor where everything went and then asked if they could do an activity together. The supervisor agreed. They worked together for a few minutes, which gave them a chance to talk. The supervisor asked him if he understood what control was and he didn't. They talked about self-control and things that we couldn't control, like the weather. He reminded the child that the classroom was in his control and that he could really be helpful if he wanted to. With a new understanding of the class and himself, the child became the classroom helper.

He voluntarily helped everybody clean and put their toys away before each transition time. He stopped taking toys from kids and started helping them. He was a very intelligent child who had started conflicts in order to feel a sense of control. That is how powerful conflict is and how it can be used to create chaos; therefore, we must learn how to use conflict to end chaos and create peace.

The teacher lost her job because she extended the conflicts that the child had created. When a customer comes into a store wanting to start a conflict, be

Mindful Sales

the person who ends it. Find out what the customer needs by listening carefully and "reading between the lines". Let's use an example:

Customer – "I saw that you repair boots on your website and I drove all the way over here to get these boots repaired but the guy in the boot department says that you don't repair boots. So, I just wasted my morning for no reason and where am I supposed to get these boots fixed?"

Employee – "I apologize for that. I'll have the manager look at the website and make sure that gets removed. I understand – it totally sucks to drive all the way here only to find out you can't get your boots fixed. I can't fix your boots but if you give me a minute I'll get you the phone number and address of a local shop that does repair boots." - This employee had done his research and knew how to meet the customer's needs.

Customer – "Well, alright."

Employee – "O.K., great! I'll be right back." - The employee goes to the phone book and finds the number and address of a local boot repair shop, writes them down and brings the paper back to the customer. Customer – "Okay. Well, I guess I'll give 'em a try, then."

Employee – "Great! I hope it works out for you and, again, I apologize for the inconvenience this morning."

Customer – "That's alright. It's not your fault but you really should get someone to take that off of your website."

Employee – "Oh, I will. Thank you for bringing that to our attention. We need people to be honest with us like that so that we can make things right. I really appreciate that and your patience."

Customer – "Hey, no problem. Thanks for helping me out."

That interaction actually happened in a store that one of the authors worked at – the website error was real and the customer started out really angry but left really happy. Guess where he bought his next pair of boots – from that store. And guess what sales person he requested – that's right, the one who helped him on the day that he felt completely lied to and let down by the store. Until that sales person stepped in, was honest and was able to see the conflict as an opportunity to help and to grow - that changed everything. The employee heard that the customer was upset but he "read between the lines" and realized that the customer actually just wanted his boots repaired until he could afford a new pair. He sought to understand the customer and that ended the conflict. Everybody wants to be understood.

Once you understand what the needs of your customer are then you can take the next step, as that employee did, and offer assistance. If the company that you're working for can provide the service or product that the customer needs, then that's great. If the company can't then help the customer by providing helpful referrals or suggestions. Assistance can come in many forms and can be very helpful in turning dirty conflicts into healthy soil with fruitful rewards. Showing such integrity and humility will keep customers coming back.

Mindful Sales

Chapter 8

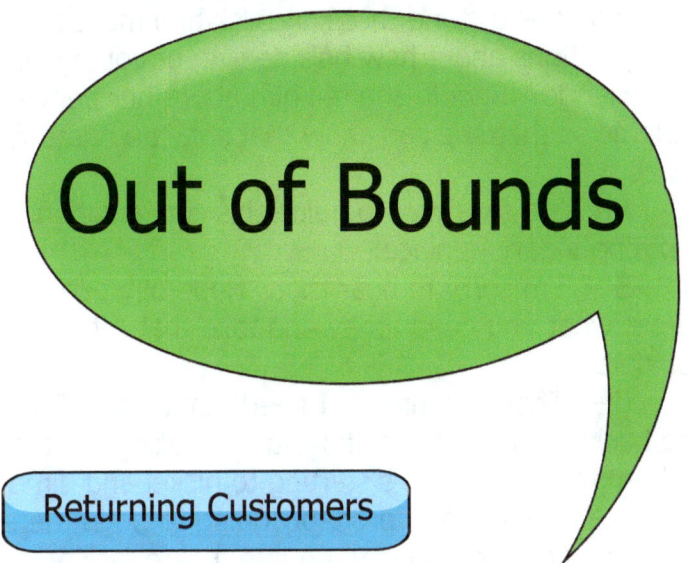

Out of Bounds

Returning Customers

Returning customers are important to sales people; especially those who receive commissions. Knowing your customer, understanding your customer, leads to more sales but the lines between "friend", "acquaintance" and "customer" can get blurred. Setting and keeping a clear boundary with your customer will lead to a long term, professional relationship.

Consider this scenario in which the customer is "C" and the sales person is "S":

    C – "Hey, S, how ya been?"

    S – "Great! How about you?"

    C – "Could be better. My dad's in the hospital and my mom just passed away last month."

This is an important point to notice in the conversation. What do you think that the sales person should say next?

How would she keep a boundary in place and still show some empathy? Should she give the customer her number and tell him to call anytime that he needs to talk? Should she stand there and ask him more personal questions about how he's dealing or coping with the challenge? Should she tell him about her personal problems so that she can show that she can relate to his?

Here's a safe way to guide this conversation and keep a boundary in place:

S – "I'm sorry to hear that. Hopefully I can help you get what you need today and take that off of your shoulders."

C – "That'd be great. I need a new car. Traveling back and forth to the hospital is costing me too much in gas and my car's starting to nickel and dime me to death. Plus, he's probably going to be in there for a while and then have to go into a care facility, which is even farther away."

Here, again, is a good time to guide the conversation and keep it focused on what you can, as a sales person, help him with – getting a fuel efficient car so that he can see his father.

S – "I understand. I can help you with that. We have five new models that get really great gas mileage. Would you like to see them?"

Keeping the conversation focused on helping in the only way that you can, as a professional, will set a boundary and keep it intact. The customer will walk away feeling understood and helped and you will walk away knowing that you were helpful in the right way at the right time. You have integrity and you prove it by keeping these boundaries.

Integrity also requires honesty. If you don't

have a car in his price range that has good fuel economy, then let him know that and offer suggestions. Maybe you know that your manager is going to an auction the next week and you can ask the manager to look for a car that will fit his needs. Maybe you can let him know that you get trade-ins every day and you'll call him if anything comes in that will work for him. Maybe you have to tell him that you can't help him that day – it's better than deceiving him and he will respect you for your honesty.

If you do have some way to help him and offer assistance, be sure to follow-up. Call him if your manager finds a car at auction. Call him if a trade-in comes in that he can afford. Call him with any information that can help him to get the car that he needs. Following up in this way lets him know that you care without getting involved in his private life or bringing him into yours. The relationship is professional and keeping it that way ensures that he will be back and, probably, refer you to friends and family when they need a new vehicle. This type of integrity also creates great customer service, which is really what a sales person provides.

Chapter 9

...is the foundation of sales. Customer service has a few important components.
1. Attentiveness
2. Communication
3. Patience
4. Understanding
5. Knowledge

These five components are repeated throughout this book, in different ways, for a reason -they build healthy relationships. Taking the stance of a helpful, honest and hard-working person will help you to help the customer and that's all that any customer really wants. Pay attention to your customer. Communicate clearly and ask clarifying questions. Be patient when a customer is unsure or unclear about what she wants or needs. Understand her needs or desires. Provide knowledge to help the customer make an informed purchase that she will be happy with in the long run.

    Offering assistance is also part of this stance. Show that you're prepared to work for the customer. Show that you're willing to help. And remember to follow through with any assistance that you offer. This will create a relationship built on respect and trust. Reading about this is easy but how does one go about keeping this stance during stressful or boring or just plain old difficult days?

Mindful Sales

Chapter 10

In Focus

Any stance...

...can only be held in the moment. You can think about your basketball stance or how you're going to stand while giving a speech in the near future but the stance, itself, is something that only exists in the moment. When you are standing in front of a customer then your idea of having a customer in front of you is gone and the actual customer is there, right? It's the same with your stance. In each moment, how are you thinking, acting and/or speaking?

For a moment, we return to the beginning of the book to understand this aspect. Remember reading, "Your entire first few years were spent in a state of deep mindfulness as you focused entirely on learning to walk and talk."? Well, at some point, most of us lose this focus and our thoughts begin to bounce around like loose ping-pong balls in our minds. It's okay – it's normal – but it doesn't have to be that way. We can

Mindful Sales

return to that "stance" that we had as children and recall that ability. It just takes practice.

Adolfo began to practice at age 16. He was defensive and scared. He changed his stance at age seventeen. He worked full time, completed high school and then college with little support. The new stance that he'd adopted was one of understanding. He found kindness to be a strength, understanding to be a form of protection and compassion and acceptance as forms of courage. He learned how to be mindful from teachers, grandparents, books and even children. He watched and observed. He paid attention to what worked and didn't work and began paying attention to his own stance. How was he approaching situations? How was he understanding others? What could he do differently in order to have a happier, healthier life?

Questioning one's self in these ways helps to build a strong, solid stance in the same way that a baseball player practices his batting stance over and over again. These questions are practice pitches, aimed at seeing our ability to concentrate and focus. Some people like to write in order to work through these types of questions, others may draw while thinking about such things and many just sit quietly in mediation or thoughtful stillness. Barbara has recently experienced mindfulness as a concept but, like most people, has been mindful at many times in her life. Understanding that customers had a "comfrort zone" was a mindful moment in her life. Now, she uses prayer to find peace. Whatever approach works for you is fine as long as you are learning one thing – stillness.

The stance is really about stillness of the mind. Imagine a cat stalking its prey. The cat can hold perfectly still for as long as it takes. All animals spend much of their time doing little or nothing at all. We humans have forgotten how to do this but it is built into our DNA. We've come up with this "idea", this "concept", called "laziness". That idea has created the delusion that moving quickly and looking busy means productivity. Research is proving that people who are too busy are less productive and, of course, people who are rarely busy are less productive. We want to find the middle ground. Our minds can be "too busy" and, therefore, less productive.

Stillness of the mind creates a solid stance. When a customer is irritated, frustrated or upset a sales person with a still mind can help to transform that energy into something fruitful. Let's look at a day when a customer tried to return a machete for "manufacturing defects". The blade had obviously been slammed into rock or metal. It was bent, chipped and seriously abused. The customer insisted on being given a new one and the sales person who was helping her had a very busy mind. Layers of stress built up between the two and the sales person came to ask a co-worker for help. The co-worker was a very mindful person. He approached the customer and held the machete quietly between them, observing the damage.

That few seconds of silence between them helped to calm her down just a little. He then asked her, "What do you think could do this to a steel blade?" She said that she didn't know but that a machete should last longer than just one job. He agreed with her and asked if she had been using the machete. She said, "No, my nephew was using it to clear the land behind our house." He responded, "Oh. That's nice that he can help you with all of that hard work." She calmed down a little bit more.

Next, he suggested that they try something. He went to an old fixture in the store and hit the blade very hard against a metal bar. It made a small "ding" in the edge of the blade. Seeing that the blade was strong and hard to chip or bend she suddenly said, "I wonder if he was hitting rocks with it." She admitted that they also had metal fence posts around the property and said, "Well, it probably was his fault. I guess I'll have to get a new one and tell him to be more careful." He suggested that she get a better tool and showed her one that was twice as thick as the machete. It also cost twice as much as the machete, was twice as efficient for the type of brush that she was having cut, and would last twice as long as machete. She happily paid for the better tool.

A few weeks later she came in, thanked him, and bought another tool for her son because it had worked so well! Having a solid, compassionate stance rooted in reality had allowed the sales person to help the customer to see the reality that the tool had been abused and was not defective. That first move toward understanding turned the entire situation from a kind of crisis into a higher sale and a happy customer who returned grateful and wanting more. That customer moved from being very unhappy and uncomfortable to being comfortable. He'd helped to create what Barbara calls the "comfort zone" for her in our store, which made all of us feel great!

Chapter 11

The Comfort Zone

Creating...

...a "comfort zone" for the customer really works. The standard sales model involves pressuring people and it has been shown to work, but at what cost? Companies using that model are upsetting people every day. Now, there's an alternative.

The new model is Mindful Sales. Being mindful of what the customer needs, his or her mood at the time and your own responses helps to create the comfort zone. In that zone, the customer feels comfortable enough to make her own choice. There's a feeling of freedom and security that automatically creates a strong relationship. People will ask your name and come back in and ask to work with you because they feel safe and comfortable with you. They know that you'll provide information and let them make their own choices without feeling pressured into buying something that they don't really want or need. They'll know

Mindful Sales

this at a subconscious level. They'll know the feeling that they get when they're around you. Mindfulness teaches you to concentrate your attention. When a customer is in front of you, and you are mindful, that customer is the most important person at that time and place. Your focus and attention create a sort of calm in the storm of daily life.

It begins with being aware of yourself and then that awareness expands out, like an energy surge, into the area around you and effects anybody near you. Co-workers, family and friends also benefit from practicing this way of life. Creating comfort zones for people is an act of compassion. It's easy to take our stress out on others, make them uncomfortable or just be mean. If something is easy, that means it doesn't take much strength, right?

Conversely, it's more challenging to remain calm, solid and consistent. Challenges make us stronger. Keep the concept of strength clear. Strength is not just a physical trait. It's also a state of mind. The solid mind is the strong mind. Take on the challenge to learn to breathe, to focus and concentrate on the person in front of you, on learning information about the products that you sell and on how you're feeling at any given moment so that you can accept yourself and others. This simple way of life will help you to help others, who will, in turn, help others. Creating a comfort zone wherever you go, especially at work where you interact with many, many people, will help to create comfort zones throughout your community and the world.

The world is whatever is in front of you at the moment. The world is whatever is in your mind. The world is not so much what you make of it but is actually just what it is – the world at that moment. It's always changing. Everybody sees the world in their own way. Everybody experiences life in their own way. Your job, as a sales person, is to understand that and to help every different person find what they need or want at that particular moment in time. Thinking only helps until it's time to take action, then you need focus and concentration. If you know the product, and can listen to the customer, then you can create the comfort zone! Winning, in sports, generally means getting the highest score, right? Winning in sales means helping people to make informed choices that lead to contentment. If a customer walks away content, then that's a win! That customer will tell others and they, too, will come to see you when they need something. You create a recurring cycle of kindness and support and we need more of that in the business world. It works, so what are you waiting for? Today is the day, now is the time and mindful sales is the key.

Namaste!